I0532108

CATECHISM AND BAPTISM

URIM
BOOKS

CATECHISM AND BAPTISM

Published by Urim Books (Representative: Seongnam Vin)
235-3, Guro-dong 3, Guro-gu, Seoul, Korea
www.urimbooks.com

All rights reserved. This book or parts thereof may not
be reproduced in any form, stored in a retrieval system,
or transmitted in any form or by any means, electronic,
mechanical, photocopying, recording or otherwise, without
prior written permission of the publisher.

Copyright©2011 by Urim Books
ISBN: 978-89-7557- 492-4
Translation Copyright©2010 by Dr. Esther K. Chung. Used
by permission.

First published in March 12, 1993 by Publication
Department of the United Holiness Church of Jesus Christ

First Edition: November 2011

Edited by Geumsun Vin, Education Department of the
United Holiness Church of Jesus Christ
Designed by Editorial Bureau of Urim Books
Printed by Yewon Printing Company
For more information contact: urimbook@hotmail.com or
s8225237@hanmail.net

Foreword

In commemoration of the 20th anniversary of The United Holiness Church of Jesus Christ and according to the requests of approximately a ten thousand branch and associative churches all over the world, I am delighted to have the publication of this book *Catechism and Baptism*.

Only when children learn and acquire various kinds of knowledge and instructions during their growth can they become equipped with proper qualifications to live lives of healthy and social people. It is the same in faith. New believers who have just accepted the Lord can become spiritual warriors only when they are provided with the knowledge of the spirit and the instructions of the Lord that are necessary for successful lives in the Lord.

This book is a compilation of the teachings every believer must read and abide by to be baptized in the name of God the Trinity and to lead a proper Christian life. It includes not only whatever believers in Christ must keep and avoid but introduction to the Old and New Testaments, biblical doctrines, and church creed as well.

Many examples of the questions and the answers new believers must study in preparation for baptism are contained in this book. It is for them to have the assurance of salvation and to lay the foundation in the life worthy for a member of the church, the body of the Christ. The study of those examples helps them more easily understand fundamentals of a Christian life, the Bible, doctrines, and church creed.

This guidebook can be used in any church to help new believers to prepare for the baptism ceremony, and each church can choose various questions from the examples. New believers of every church, prior to being baptized, must study this book and go through the regulated process in order to have the proper heart and attitude for baptism.

Those who have completed the general catechism or catechism for baptism can attend the general catechism completion ceremony or baptism ceremony, and then they are registered as a catechismal member or a baptized member. Those who are baptized can then be entitled to receive the rights as a regular church member and are supposed to perform their God-given duties, and accordingly, they can receive God's blessings.

May each and every believer who studies this book lay a firm foundation in his/her faith and contribute to church growth, in the name of our Lord Jesus Christ I pray!

March 2011

Rev. Dr. Jaerock Lee
Chairman, The United Holiness Church of Jesus Christ

Table of Contents

Foreword

Part 1

CHRISTIAN LIFE

Categories and Duties of Church Members

1. Categories of Church Members

The church members are categorized into three kinds of groups: churchgoers, novice believers and baptized believers.

1) Registered Members

"Registered Members" refers to the ones who attend the worship services with a desire to become a Christian and whose names are registered on the church members' list. In order to become Christians they have to accept Jesus Christ, listen to the Word of God by attending the worship service and learn how to lead a proper Christian life.

2) Catechismal Members

"Catechismal Members" refer to those who are studying to become Christians. When those members who are 13 years of age and older have repented of their sins and accepted the Lord, and try to live a faithful Christian life, thereby having the evidences of their faith, they can finish the catechism and their names can be registered in the 'Catechismal Members List'. In order to become a true and faithful Christian, they have to attend worship services on a regular basis and to lead a proper Christian life by obeying the Word of God.

3) Baptized Members

Four to five months after having become catechismal members, those who have the evidences of being born again as God's children can complete the catechism for baptism and receive the baptism to be registered in the "Baptized Members List." They are entitled to take part in the decision-making process of the church as one of the members of the body of the church. They accept the duty to offer dedication and service to the kingdom of God and the church.

For the sake of the kingdom and righteousness of God, all those who have become registered members should fulfill their duties and responsibilities as recorded in the Bible, and have the qualifications of God's holy children.

1) They have to diligently attend the official worship services and worship God in truth and in spirit.

The official services are the Sunday Morning Service, Sunday Evening Service, Wednesday Evening Service, and the Friday All-night Service. The worship service is the ceremony to acknowledge the living God and thank and worship God for His love and grace. God is seeking true worshippers who worship Him in spirit and in truth and through His Word He blesses those worshippers who sincerely worship Him with all their heart, mind, and soul.

2) They have to try to read and study the Bible.

Our faith will increase and we will lead a proper Christian life as we come to understand the will of God while reading, hearing, and learning the Word of God.

3) They have to try their best to live by the Word of God and pray.

Prayer is the breathing of our spirit. It is how we have conversation with God, who is spirit, and it is a means to receive God's power. Any believer who wishes to live in accordance with the will of God must pray to God.

4) They have to rejoice always, pray without ceasing, and give thanks in everything.

We can rejoice always just for the fact that we have gained possession of the everlasting kingdom of Heaven with faith in Jesus Christ. We must pray unceasingly in order to receive the help of God the Almighty, and we are able to give thanks in everything because we believe God causes all things to work for the good.

5) They have to show their dedication to the church ministry and missionary works and give offerings to God unsparingly.

Believing that everything belongs to God, but He entrusts everything to us as stewards, we must serve God with our body and possessions. Especially believers must sincerely give to God a tenth of all their income, and not begrudgingly or under compulsion.

6) They have to fervently preach the gospel and evangelize others with gifts given to them from above.

It is because God counts a single soul more valuable than the whole universe and wants us to become the Lord's witnesses who spread the gospel in and out of season.

Chapter 2

Obligations of Church Members

1. Ten Commandments

Each nation has its own law and each organization has its rules. In the same way, the believers in God have the laws in the kingdom of God and the laws are called the 'commandments.' In 1 John 5:3 we find recorded, *"For this is the love of God, that we keep His commandments; and His commandments are not burdensome."* Keeping the commandments of God is the proof of loving God and the shortcut to receiving His blessings.

The summation of all the commandments recorded in the Bible is the Ten Commandments (Exodus 20:3-17). The Ten Commandments can be listed in two categories. One is concerned with the love for God and the other concerning the love for our neighbors.

1) *"You shall have no other gods before Me."*
2) *"You shall not make for yourself an idol, or any likeness of what is in heaven above or on the earth beneath or in the water under the earth. You shall not worship them or serve them."*
3) *"You shall not take the name of the LORD your God in vain."*
4) *"Remember the Sabbath day, to keep it holy."*
5) *"Honor your father and your mother."*
6) *"You shall not murder."*
7) *"You shall not commit adultery."*
8) *"You shall not steal."*
9) *"You shall not bear false witness against your neighbor."*
10) *"You shall not covet your neighbor's house."*

2. Keep the Lord's Day Holy

The Lord's Day refers to Sunday symbolizing the day when the Lord Jesus broke the power of death and resurrected. It also refers to the Sabbath day that God blessed and sanctified so that we might take a true rest in the Lord. When we keep the Lord's

Day holy and take true rest in the Lord, we can also receive the blessing of the prosperity of our soul.

1) Keeping the Lord's Day is the will of God. It is also the proof that we recognize the spiritual authority of God.

In the Book of Genesis chapter 2 verses 1-3 we find that when God created the heavens and the earth, and everything in them, He completed His work of creation in six days and then He rested on the seventh day. He blessed and sanctified the seventh day. In Exodus 20:8, God commanded His people to remember the Sabbath day and keep it holy. Thus, when we remember and keep the Lord's Day holy according to the command of God, it can be deemed that we recognize the spiritual authority of God and thus God rejoices and blesses us.

2) Concerning the Sabbath of the Old Testament and the Lord's Day of the New Testament

In Old Testament times the last day of the 7-day creation, namely Saturday was kept as the Sabbath. However, in New Testament times Sunday is celebrated as the Sabbath because Jesus Christ resurrected on Sunday.

Human beings corrupted and came to fall into death due to sins, thereby not being able to go into true rest of God (Genesis 3).

Therefore, God sent His one and only Son, Jesus to the earth, whom He had prepared since before the ages. He had Him redeem all men from their sins by His blood and opened the door to salvation for all men (Galatians 3:13).

Jesus was hung and died on the cross on Friday, and resurrected on the third day, which was Sunday (Matthew 28:1). He became the firstfruits of resurrection (1 Corinthians 15:20) and the Lord of the Sabbath, so that anyone can now enjoy true rest with faith and hope of resurrection. Since then the believers keep Sunday as the Sabbath (1 Corinthians 16:2) calling it "the Lord's Day."

3) Ways to keep the Lord's Day holy and the blessings that accompany it

We find recorded in Exodus 20:8-10 that we should labor and do all our works for six days and rest on the Lord's Day in the Lord. We can enjoy true rest when we have not only physical rest but also spiritual rest.

That's why on the Lord's Day, first of all, we should not do any worldly work but come to church to worship God in spirit and in truth. Secondly, we should stay far away from worldly pleasures and entertainments and live a godly life during the entire day. We should keep our thoughts and minds blameless, and make our body, clothes and house tidy and clean beforehand. On the

Lord's Day, we should dedicate the day to the Lord with thanks and joy without committing evils.

Thirdly, we should attend not only Sunday Morning Service but also Sunday Evening Service to keep the Lord's Day holy, and worship God in spirit and in truth during the worship services. And we should love the temple of God and make it holy in spirit and flesh. Fourthly, we should neither commit the deeds of selling and buying, nor share any worldly conversations for our benefit in the sanctuary (Nehemiah 13:15-22).

Thus, when we glorify God and take true rest in accordance with the will of God on the Lord's Day, God will be delighted and bless us. As our soul prospers, He will let everything go well with us and make us healthy, and cause everything to work for the good during the week.

3. Whole Tithe and Offerings

"Giving tithe" is the decree of God commanding us to give God a tenth of our income, and it is the proof of recognizing that all material things belong to God who created the heavens and the earth and everything in them. God wants us to give Him whole tithe and offerings.

1) "Giving whole tithes" is the will of God and the deed of recognizing God's authority over all material things.

Malachi 3:8-9 explains us that the reason why the sons of Israel were cursed was because they distanced themselves from the laws of God by not giving whole tithe and offerings to God. Whole tithe refers to a tenth of the total of our income including income through business, work and other ways.

Even though we have labored and gained all gains through our toil, effort and sweat, we should acknowledge that the income does not belong to us, but to God who is the Master of the heavens and the earth and all things in them and who committed the incomes to us. Thus, we acknowledge that we are merely stewards, and He asks us to return to Him but a tenth of that income.

2) The ways to give God our whole tithe are as follows:

First, we should give tithe from the whole of our income.

Second, we should set our tithe apart from other offerings.

Third, we should give our tithe to the church that provides us with spiritual food.

Fourth, each of us should give tithe under our individual name.

Fifth, we have to give our tithe at least once a month.

Sixth, even those who don't have regular, monetary income from a job should still give tithe for the meals they are treated to, gifts they receive, and other in-kind income.

Seventh, the tithe must be set apart from our income prior to other expenditures.

3) Offerings refer to all kinds of offerings given to God in general.

When we give God offerings, we should give offerings that are without defect; we should give the first of all our produce; we should give with thanksgiving, and not begrudgingly or under compulsion; the offerings we have vowed to give God should not be either annulled or exchanged with others; and the offerings must be carried to the pulpit and be prayed on by the preacher through laying of hand.

These offerings are categorized into several types including the Offering of Thanksgiving, the Ordination Offering for the God-given duty and title, the Sin Offering for the sins we have committed, the Peace Offering for the reconciliation with God, etc. We should not give thanks to God only with words, but also give Him offerings in the deeds of faith. Then God will joyfully accept them and pay us back with appropriate blessings.

The tithes and offerings belong to God, so nobody can use them at their personal discretion. They must be used through the financial organization of the church in accordance with the will of God.

4) When we give the whole tithe and offerings, God's blessing will come upon us.

In Malachi 3:10 God promises us that if we bring the whole tithe into the storehouse of God He will pour out for us a blessing until it overflows. God even tells us to test Him if He will fulfill His promise. He wishes that through the test of tithes, even those who doubt His promise and reluctantly and sparingly give tithes will come to realize, repent, and obey with faith and then reach the boundary of salvation and receive blessing. 2 Corinthians 9:6-7 says that he who sows sparingly will also reap sparingly, and he who sows bountifully will also reap bountifully.

When we understand the will of God correctly and lead a proper Christian life according to His will, we can please God and receive all blessings God promises to give us. The believers in the God who always keeps His promises and who is love itself should give God the whole tithes and offerings.

Chapter 3
Prohibitions for Church Members

Believers as children of God have the duties they have to keep, and they also have the things that they should avoid.

1. We should not take the holy name of God in vain before men, and neither have any words or deeds of denial and betrayal.

2. We should not believe the Bible partially and neither delete, exclude or criticize the revelations of God in interpretating the Bible.

3. We should abstain from any worldly business or labor and never engage in the acts of selling and buying on the Lord's Day.

4. We should neither sing worldly songs that are vulgar or

in poor taste, nor should we dance in a secular manner that is indecent or licentious. We should not go to the places of entertainment or amusement that promote the opportunity to sin.

5. We should abstain from imprudent expressions, violent language, slandering words, abusing words, reckless judgment, condemnations, meaningless words, immoral words, lies, and all kinds of useless words.

6. We should not repay evil for evil, but have regard for good things all the time. We should not sue one another in the courts of law. We should not coerce another to do anything that we would not be willing to do.

7. There must not be either money exchange or a guarantor for the other's debts among the believers at all.
"Do not be among those who give pledges, among those who become guarantors for debts." (Proverbs 22:26)

8. We must not commit evident works of the flesh.
"Now the deeds of the flesh are evident, which are: immorality, impurity, sensuality, idolatry, sorcery, enmities,

strife, jealousy, outbursts of anger, disputes, dissensions, factions, envying, drunkenness, carousing, and things like these, of which I forewarn you, just as I have forewarned you, that those who practice such things will not inherit the kingdom of God." (Galatians 5:19-21)

9. We must never commit any sin that leads to death.

"If anyone sees his brother committing a sin not leading to death, he shall ask and God will for him give life to those who commit sin not leading to death. There is a sin leading to death; I do not say that he should make request for this." (1 John 5:16)

<Sins Leading to Death>

1. Speaking against, opposing, and disgracing the Holy Spirit
   (Matthew 12:31-32; Mark 3:29; Luke 12:10)
2. Crucifying the Lord again and putting Him to open shame
   (Hebrews 6:4-6)
3. Continuing in willful sinning after receiving the knowledge of the truth
   (Hebrews 10:26-27)

Matthew 12:31-32

"Therefore I say to you, any sin and blasphemy shall be forgiven people, but blasphemy against the Spirit shall not be forgiven. Whoever speaks a word against the Son of Man, it shall be forgiven him; but whoever speaks against the Holy Spirit, it shall not be forgiven him, either in this age or in the age to come."

Mark 3:29

"But whoever blasphemes against the Holy Spirit never has forgiveness, but is guilty of an eternal sin."

Luke 12:10

"And everyone who speaks a word against the Son of Man, it will be forgiven him; but he who blasphemes against the Holy Spirit, it will not be forgiven him."

Hebrews 6:4-6

"For in the case of those who have once been enlightened and have tasted of the heavenly gift and have been made partakers of the Holy Spirit, and have tasted the good word of God and the powers of the age to come, and then have fallen away, it is impossible to renew them again to repentance, since they again crucify to themselves the Son of God and put Him to open shame."

Hebrews 10:26-27

"For if we go on sinning willfully after receiving the knowledge of the truth, there no longer remains a sacrifice for sins, but a terrifying expectation of judgment and the fury of a fire which will consume the adversaries."

Chapter 4

Marriage, Funerals, and Memorials

1. Marriage Life

Since marriage is a holy ceremony that God Himself established, a man and a woman should not decide recklessly, but be careful with regard to the decision. Those considering marriage should keep the following guidelines:

1) A believer should not marry an unbeliever.

2) When a church member wants to get married, he/she is supposed to receive counsel from his/her guidance pastor, and should not have any physical and sexual relations before marriage.

3) Parents should not force their children to get married or object to their marriage if there is no violation of the biblical teachings. The children should gain the consent from their parents or their guardians.

4) The believers' wedding should be conducted by a pastor. When the pastor is invited to officiate the wedding ceremony, he/she should allow the couple to have the wedding after confirmation of the appropriateness of the wedding.

5) In no other case should married couples be divorced except that one spouse be forced to renounce their salvation by the other spouse.

If possible, God does not want married couples to get divorced, but to make a happy family.

If they are faced with situations in which they have to consider divorce, they might want to live seprately for some time and pray. It is very important for married people to try their best for the salvation of their spouses and children.

"But to the rest I say, not the Lord, that if any brother has a wife who is an unbeliever, and she consents to live with him, he must not divorce her. And a woman who has an unbelieving husband, and he consents to live with her, she must not send

her husband away. For the unbelieving husband is sanctified through his wife, and the unbelieving wife is sanctified through her believing husband; for otherwise your children are unclean, but now they are holy." (1 Corinthians 7:12-14)

But the Bible tells us that if the wife has an affair with another man, it would be a legitimate reason to get a divorce (Matthew 19:9).

6) They must not have a mistress; they must not have double-marriage; and they must not marry a woman who has a husband or a man who has a wife.

2. Funeral

1) Deathbed Service

In case of the death of a believer who has accepted the Lord, his/her body is supposed to be arranged and a deathbed service to be offered to God.

2) Casket Service

The body of a dead person should be shrouded and put into a coffin, and a casket service is offered.

3) Way of Mourning

Believers should not bow down or burn incense before the body of a dead person when they go to mourn, but instead greet the remaining family and offer silent prayers.

4) Processions of Funeral

They can have a 3-day or a 5-day funeral by the decision of the family. They have to offer services when the funeral cortege leaves for the grave, and before the actual burial. They should avoid Sunday for having these services.

3. Memorial Service

In commemoration of the deceased, a memorial service can be offered to God on the date of the death of the deceased.

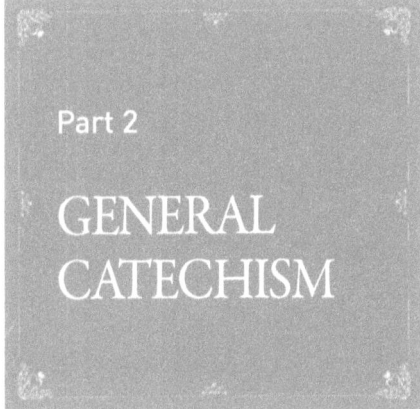

Part 2

GENERAL CATECHISM

General Catechism

Concerning Christian Life

Concerning the Bible

Concerning the Church Creed and Doctrine

Chapter 1

Concerning Christian Life

1. How long have you been attending the church?

   [number of months] months.

2. Have you kept the Lord's Day since you started attending the church?

   (Proper response to such a questions is simply, "Yes, Amen")

   [Yes]

3. Are you willing to diligently attend various worship services and other meetings held in the church?

   [Yes]

4. Are you willing to always acknowledge the church is a sacred place and to behave in a godly manner in the church and treat all facilities in it as precious?

[Yes]

5. Whom do you worship in the services?

[God]

6. What is prayer?

[Prayer is the breath of our spirit, the conversation between God and His children, and the passage way to receive God's answers and strength.]

7. To whom should we pray?

[to God]

8. In whose name do you have to pray?

[In the name of Jesus Christ]

9. How should we pray?

A) On a regular basis
B) Kneeling down
C) Crying out

D) From the bottom of heart

E) With faith and love

F) In accordance with God's will

G) Earnestly and fervently

10. What is a hymn and in what manner should hymns be sung?

[The hymnal is a book that is a compilation of various songs to praise God, and they should be sung with reverent fear and sincerity.]

11. Are you reading and studying the Scripture?

[Yes]

12. Are you willing to obey and follow the teachings and directions of the church?

[Yes]

13. Do you understand smoking and drinking are not in accordance with the will of God and abstain from them?

[Yes]

14. Are you keeping yourself from worshiping idols, relying on fortunetellers, and visiting sorcerers?

[Yes]

15. Do you refrain from enjoying gambling and other unwholesome forms of worldly entertainment?

[Yes]

16. Are you willing to stay away from money-lending business and usury?

[Yes]

17. Do you honor your parents in the Lord?

[Yes]

18. Are you willing to encourage your family to attend the church?

[Yes]

19. What is your church's name?

[_____ Church]

20. Which parish and which mission group in church do you belong to?

[_____ Parish _____ Mission]

21. Do you believe the church is the gathering of the people who have been called by God?

[Yes]

22. Have you decided to believe in God until your last moment?

[Yes]

Chapter 2

Concerning the Bible

1. What is the sacred scriptural book of Christianity?

   [The Bible]

2. Into what two major sections is the Bible divided?

   [The Old Testament and the New Testament]

3. How many books constitute the Bible?

   [Sixty-six books: 39 books of the Old Testament and 27 books of the New Testament]

4. What is the Bible?

   [The Bible is the recording of the living Word of God.]

5. Who recorded the Bible and how was it done?

[God-chosen people recorded it in the inspiration of the Spirit of God.] (2 Timothy 3:16)

6. Which book of the Bible records God's creation of the heavens and the earth and mankind?

[Genesis]

7. Which book of the Bible records the Ten Commandments Moses received from God?

[Exodus]

8. On which day did God make man during His creation of the heavens and the earth and everything in them?

[On the sixth day] (Genesis 1:27)

9. According to the Bible, who were the original ancestors of all mankind?

[Adam and Eve]

10. How did God make the first man, Adam?

[God formed the first man of dust from the ground, and breathed the breath of life into his nostrils, and then the man became a living being.]

11. What kind of fruit did Adam and Eve eat so that they disobeyed the Word of God?

[The fruit from the tree of the knowledge of good and evil]

12. After God formed every beast of the field and every bird of the sky, who gave them each an individual name?

[Adam]

13. Who were the sons that Adam and Eve begat on earth as recorded in the Bible?

[Cain, Abel and Seth]

14. Who walked with God for 300 years and then was taken up into Heaven alive?

[Enoch]

15. Who was called "a righteous, blameless man" and made the ark before the Great Flood?

[Noah]

16. Who was called the "Father of Faith"?

[Abraham]

17. Whom did Abraham beget at the age of 100?

[Isaac]

18. Who were the two sons Isaac fathered?

[Esau and Jacob]

19. Who sold his birthright to his younger brother for a bowl of lentil stew?

[Esau]

20. How many sons did Jacob beget as the 'Father of Israel'?

[Twelve sons]

21. Which son of Jacob was sold into slavery in Egypt but blessed to become the ruler of the land after the Pharaoh?

[Joseph]

22. Who led the people of Israel from the bondage of Egypt by the calling of God?

[Moses]

23. Which books of the Bible are called the 'Pentateuch" or the "Five Books of Moses"?

[Genesis, Exodus, Leviticus, Numbers, and Deuteronomy]

24. Where did Moses receive the Ten Commandments from God?

[On the Mountain of Sinai]

25. What was the land that God promised the sons of Israel as their inheritance?

[The Land of Canaan]

26. Who led the sons of Israel into the Promised Land as the successor to Moses?

[Joshua]

27. Who was the last judge of Israel who anointed Saul as the king of Israel?

[Samuel]

28. Which king of Israel gained the greatest favor from God in Old Testament times?

[David]

29. What does the name 'Jesus' mean?

["The one who will save His people from their sins"]

30. Where was Jesus born?

[In Bethlehem, Judea]

31. Where did Jesus live in His childhood?

[In Nazareth, Galilee]

32. Which books of the Bible testify to the earthly life and ministry of Jesus?

[The Four Gospels of Matthew, Mark, Luke and John]

33. How many years ago did Jesus come into this world?

[The standard calendar we are using is based on the birth of Jesus. So Jesus was born _____ years ago.]

34. How was Jesus conceived in the virgin Mary?

[Jesus was conceived in the virgin Mary by the power of the Holy Spirit.]

35. What is the first sign Jesus performed at Cana, Galilee?

[The miracle of turning water into wine]

36. How many disciples did Jesus have?

[Twelve]

37. How did Jesus die?

[He was crucified to redeem all men from their sins]

38. Which disciple of Jesus betrayed Him and sold Him out for thirty silver coins?

[Judas Iscariot]

39. How long did Jesus hang on the cross?

[Six hours]

40. What is the reason that Jesus was nailed through His hands and feet?

[It was to redeem us from our sins we commit with our hands and feet.]

41. Why was Jesus crowned with thorns?

[It was to redeem us from our sins we commit in our thoughts.]

42. Jesus died and was buried. On which day after His burial was He resurrected from the dead?

[He resurrected on the third day.]

43. What did Jesus Christ do after He resurrected?

[He presented Himself to His apostles for 40 days and then ascended into Heaven.]

44. Who knows the hour and the day of the Lord's Second Advent?

[Only God the Father] (Matthew 24:36; Mark 13:32)

45. Which book of the New Testament records the history of the acts of the apostles?

[The Book of Acts]

46. Which apostle preached the gospel of Jesus Christ to the Gentiles with manifestations of God's powerful miracles even though he was not an original disciple of Jesus?

[The Apostle Paul]

47. Which book of the Bible records the revelations and prophecies about the future written by the Apostle John?

[The Book of Revelation]

48. What is the wages of sin according to the Bible?

[Death] (Romans 6:23)

49. Which right is given us by God when we accept Jesus Christ as our Savior?

[The right to become the children of God] (John 1:12)

Concerning the Church
Creed and Doctrine

1. From when and until when does God exist?

   [From everlasting to everlasting] (Psalm 90:2)

2. How many gods are there in the world that we have to worship?

   [Only one God]

3. Do you believe God created the heavens and the earth by His Word?

   [Yes]

4. Do you believe Heaven and Hell really exist?

   [Yes]

5. By whose name can we be saved?

[By the name of Jesus Christ]

6. What is salvation?

["Salvation" is to be saved through faith in Jesus Christ from death caused by sins and receive an eternal life.]

7. What does Christ mean?

["Christ" means "God's Anointed One" referring to the Messiah.]

8. Do you believe there is salvation by no other name but Jesus Christ?

[Yes]

9. What gift does God give to those who accept Jesus Christ as the Savior?

[The Holy Spirit]

10. Do you acknowledge and believe the Apostles' Creed as your confession of faith?

[Yes]

11. What are the examples of official worship services?

[Sunday Morning Service, Sunday Evening Service, Wednesday Evening Service, and the Friday All-night Service]

12. How should we dedicate ourselves in the worship service?

[We should pay attention to every proceeding of the service from silent prayer until the Lord's Prayer or the preacher's benediction.]

13. What is meant by the Lord's Day?

[It is our Sabbath that God blessed and sanctified, on which we can have a true rest in the Lord.]

14. What is the name of the denomination to which our church belongs?

[The United Holiness Church of Jesus Christ]

15. What is the five-fold Gospel of Holiness, which is the five main doctrines of our church?

[Regeneration; Sanctification; Divine Healing; Resurrection; and Second Advent of the Lord]

16. What festivities do we observe in our church?

    [Easter (Passover); Feast of Harvest; Thanksgiving (Feast of Ingathering); Christmas]

17. Do you believe the Bible is the absolute, errorless and everlastingly persistent Word of God?

    [Yes]

18. In what aspects are men different from animals?

    [Unlike animals that do not have spirit, men were created in the image of God with spirit, soul, and body, and thus they can fear God.]

19. Do you believe that Jesus is God in origin, but came down to earth in human body to redeem us from our sins?

    [Yes]

20. Will you refuse heretical sects that deny the Triune God or the fact that Jesus came to this earth in the flesh, was crucified, and resurrected; and will you keep yourself away from meaningless religious disputes with such people?

    [Yes]

21. Do you believe in the Second Advent of the Lord?

[Yes]

22. When will the Great White Throne Judgment be held?

[It will be held after the Millennium Kingdom comes to an end.]

23. How long will our heavenly life last?

[The kingdom of heaven is eternal, so our heavenly lives are also everlasting.]

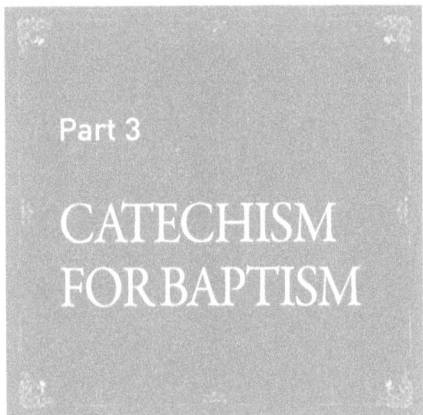

Part 3

CATECHISM FOR BAPTISM

Concerning Christian Life

Concerning the Bible

Concerning the Church Doctrine and Creed

Chapter 1

Concerning Christian Life

1. What are the qualifications to be baptized?

[They have to finish the general catechism 4 to 5 months prior to the baptism, attend church on a regular basis, and have the assurance of salvation.]

2. Have you kept the Lord's Day holy on a regular basis after the completing general catechism?

[Yes]

3. Do you read the Bible regularly every day?

[Yes]

4. Do you pray regularly every day?

[Yes]

5. Do you give God tithes and offerings of thanksgiving and for festivities?

[Yes]

6. Have you spread the gospel to other people?

[Yes]

7. After being baptized, as a member of the church are you willing to dedicate yourself to services and evangelical ministries of the church?

[Yes]

8. Are you attending the cell worship services?

[Yes]

9. Are you joining the Sunday meeting of your mission group?

[Yes]

10. Are you willing to cast off all forms of evils without compromising with the world and to accomplish the holy heart of the Lord?

[Yes]

11. How should you attend the worship service?

[We must worship God in spirit and in truth]

12. What is true repentance?

[It is to realize and acknowledge we are sinners, repent of our sins with tears and tearing heart, and to depart from sins.]

13. What is a church?

[A church is the gathering of those who have listened to the truth and gained eternal life; who obey Jesus Christ as the Head of the church; and who are taught to live the life of righteousness by the ministering pastor.]

14. What is the correct attitude in interpretating the Bible?

[All Scripture is inspired by God, and thus we must interpret it in the inspiration of the Holy Spirit through fervent prayers, and we must not interpret the revelations and prophecies with criticism.]

Chapter 2 — Concerning the Bible

1. How can we recognize the existence of God?

[Through the nature that God created (Romans 1:20) and the Bible, which is the recordings of the Word of God (2 Timothy 3:15-17)]

2. Why did God create mankind?

[To gain true children who glorify Him and are worthy to share love with Him]

3. What is the order in the Creation of the World?

[1st day: the light; 2nd day: the expanse; 3rd day: earth, seas, vegetation, plants, and trees; 4th day: the sun, the moon, and stars; 5th day: fish and birds; and 6th day: animals, cattles, and man]

4. What kind of life did God bless man to live?

[God blessed them to be fruitful, multiply and subdue the earth and rule over every living creature.]

5. What is the reason that mankind has failed to enjoy all the blessings God gave them?

[It is because of disobedience to the command of God and committing the sin of eating from the tree of the knowledge of good and evil.]

6. What kind of curse was given to the serpent that tempted Eve to sin?

[The serpent was accursed to eat dust all the days of its life and to crawl on its belly.]

7. What kinds of curses were given to the first man and woman when they ate the forbidden fruit of God?

[The man came to eat the plants of the field all the days of his life only in toil and by sweat of his face. The woman was accursed to suffer greater pain in childbirth and bringing forth children, to have a desire for her husband, and to be ruled over by him.]

8. How is the Old Testament generally categorized?

[The Pentateuch (Mosaic Law; Genesis to Deuteronomy), the Historical Books (Joshua to Esther), the Poetical Books (Job to Song of Solomon), and the Prophetical Books (Isaiah to Malachi)]

9. How is the New Testament generally categorized?

[The Four Gospels (Matthew to John), the Historical Book(Book of Acts), the Epistles (Romans to Jude) and Prophecy (The Revelation of John)]

10. What kind of test did Abraham pass to become the father of faith?

[The test of offering his only son, Isaac, as a burnt offering]

11. Where was Jacob given the name Israel?

[At the Jabbok River]

12. How did God lead the sons of Israel in the wilderness?

[God led them with a pillar of cloud by day and by a pillar of fire by night.]

13. What did God provide for the sons of Israel for their food during their life in wilderness after the exodus?

[Manna and quails]

14. What kind of person was Moses?

[Moses was more humble than any man on the face of the earth, faithful in all the household of God, and perfect enough to be able to see God face to face.]

15. Among those who were 20 years of age or older at the time of the Exodus, who were allowed to enter the land of Canaan?

[Joshua and Caleb]

16. Who was the successor to Moses? What did he do?

[He was Joshua. He led the sons of Israel into the land of Canaan, conquered the land and assigned the land to the twelve tribes.]

17. What was the era, during which the sons of Israel were ruled over by God without a king, called?

[The era of Judges]

18. What did the judges of the Bible do in the history of Israel?

[They were the rulers of theocracy who were active from the time when the sons of Israel settled in the Canaan Land until they had the monarchy.]

19. Who was the first king of Israel who disobeyed the Word of God and was finally forsaken by God?

[Saul]

20. Which king of Israel constructed the first Temple of Jerusalem and had great wisdom?

[Solomon]

21. What happened to the Kingdom of Israel after King Solomon died and his son Rehoboam came in power?

[The Kingdom was split into two kingdoms: the Northern Kingdom of Israel and the Southern Kingdom of Judah.]

22. What happened to the Northern Kingdom of Israel at the end?

[It was destroyed by Assyria.]

23. What happened to the Southern Kingdom of Judah at the end?

[It was conquered by the Babylon, and most people were taken as captives.]

24. What did the Jews do when they returned to their homeland from the 70-year captivity in Babylon?

[They rebuilt the Jerusalem Temple.]

25. What did the prophets of the Old Testament do?

[They received the Word of God and delivered it to His people.]

26. Among the four greatest prophets in the Old Testament, who prophesied on the Messiah, our Lord Jesus the most?

[Isaiah]

27. Which part of the Prophets prophesies about the Passion and crucifixion of Jesus in the most detail?

[Isaiah Chapter 53]

28. Which prophet was exiled to Babylon as a captive, but kept his faith in God and was appointed as the first commissioner after the king Darius?

[Daniel]

29. What were the three greatest festivities in the Old Testament?

[The Passover (The Feast of Unleavened Bread), The Feast of Weeks (The Feast of Harvest), and the Feast of Booths (The Feast of Ingathering)]

30. What is the difference between the Four Gospels and the Synoptic Gospels?

[The Four Books that record the life and teachings of Jesus are called the "Four Gospels" and the three of them that have the similar viewpoint are called the "Synoptic Gospels."]

31. What kind of ministry did our Lord Jesus perform as recorded in the Four Gospels?

1) He taught the will and plan of God and spread the gospel of the kingdom of heaven.

2) He destroyed the works of the enemy devil and cast out demons.

3) He healed those with illnesses and infirmities, and revived the dead.

4) He redeemed us from our sins through His crucifixion, and gave us the hope of resurrection by breaking the power of death and resurrecting.

32. Among Jesus' Twelve Disciples, who were the three that accompanied Him at the closest proximity, whom Jesus loved the most?

[Peter, James and John]

33. Which part of the Four Gospels records the Beatitudes, which is a part of Jesus' Sermon on the Mount?

[Matthew Chapter 5]

34. The magi from the east visited and worshiped the baby Jesus and gave Him three kinds of gifts. What were the three gifts?

[Gold, frankincense, and myrrh]

35. What are the proper ways to pray, which were demonstrated by Jesus as an example?

[We have to pray on a regular basis, kneeling down, in accordance with the will of God, fervently and earnestly, and crying out.]

36. Name a few of the Jesus' parables with which He taught the people.

[Parable of the Sower, Parable of the Vine, Parable of the Good Samaritan, Parable of the Talents, Parable of the Ten Virgins, Parable of a Mustard Seed, Parable of the Prodigal Son, etc]

37. Briefly recount the most famous signs that Jesus performed.

[The miracles of turning water into wine, feeding over 5,000 people with five loaves and two fish, calming down the stormy waves of the sea, walking on the water, and reviving the dead]

38. What kinds of people opposed Jesus in His time?

[High priests, priests, scribes, Pharisees, Sadducees, etc]

39. Who gave the sentence of crucifixion to Jesus?

[Pontius Pilate]

40. Where was Jesus crucified?

[At Golgotha]

41. Why is Jesus the only Savior for mankind?

1) He was a man, the nearest relative of Adam.

2) He was not a descendant of Adam.

3) He had the power to redeem men from their sins.

4) He had such love that He could sacrifice His life for sinners.

42. Why was Jesus hung on the *wooden* cross?

[To redeem us from the curse of the Law]

43. Why was Jesus flogged and why did He shed blood?

[To give us peace and release us from all kinds of diseases by solving the problem of sin that is the original cause of all diseases]

44. What does it mean by 'eating the flesh of the Son of Man'?

[The flesh of the Son of Man refers to the Word of God, which is the truth. So, 'eating the flesh of the Son of Man' means 'making our spiritual bread of the Word of God recorded in the Bible.]

45. What does it mean by 'drinking the blood of the Son of Man'?

[It means practicing with faith the Word of God that we learned.]

46. Who makes His holy temple of our body and dwells in our heart after we accept Jesus Christ?

[The Holy Spirit]

47. After Jesus' ascension into Heaven, when did Jesus' disciples first receive the Holy Spirit?

[Ten days after Jesus ascended into Heaven on the Pentecost]

48. What are the proofs of having received the Holy Spirit?

1) We try to obey God's commands.

2) We enjoy obeying the Word of God joyfully.

3) We lead a pure and godly life.

4) We begin to love brothers and sisters in Christ deep in our hearts.

5) We overcome the world with faith.

6) We come to have the assurance of salvation.

7) We become assured of receiving answers to our prayers.

8) We live a God-centered life.

49. Which of the Seven Churches received only commendation from the Lord, setting an example to the churches today?

[The church in Philadelphia]

50. In the era of the Early Churches, who was appointed as one of the twelve apostles instead of Judas Iscariot?

[Matthias]

51. Who baptized the eunuch of Ethiopia and interpreted the prophecy in the book of Isaiah for him?

[Deacon Philip]

52. Who was the apostle Peter?

[Peter was foremost of the twelve disciples. He confessed before Jesus, "You are the Christ and the Son of God." He became an apostle for the Jews, spreading the gospel with God's powerful works until he was crucified upside down.]

53. Who was the apostle Paul?

[Before he came to know about the Lord, he persecuted the believers in Jesus Christ. But after he met the Lord on the way to Damascus, he dedicated his whole life to preaching the gospel to the Gentiles. He recorded 14 books of the New Testament.]

54. What are the Nine Fruits of the Holy Spirit?

[Love, joy, peace, patience, kindness, goodness, faithfulness, gentleness, and self-control]

55. Who is the deacon who performed great signs and wonders being full of grace and power, but was stoned to death as a martyr with an accusation that he was blaspheming God?

[Stephen]

56. Which of the Epistles of the New Testament are called the 'Prison Epistles' and why?

[Ephesians, Philippians, Colossians and Philemon: They were written by Paul in his imprisonment.]

57. What are the 'Pastoral Epistles'?

[The apostle Paul wrote the letters to his beloved disciples Timothy and Titus about their ministerial works. They are the first and second Timothy, and Titus.]

58. Though a gentile, he was a devout man who feared God with all his household. He gave many alms to the Jewish people and prayed to God continually. Who is he?

[Cornelius]

59. What three elements does man consist of according to the biblical teachings?

[Spirit, soul and body] (1 Thessalonians 5:23)

60. What is the name of the heavenly dwelling place that has the throne of God and 12 pearl gates?

[New Jerusalem]

Chapter 3

Concerning the Church
Doctrine and Creed

1. What is the original sin?

[All children inherit the natures, the personalities, and appearances of their parents. Since the first man Adam committed sin, all those who are born after him are born with his sinful natures. This sinful nature is the original sin.]

2. Why did the first man Adam disobey the Word of God?

[It is because the man misused the freewill God had given him and fell into the temptations of the serpent that was under the control of Satan.]

3. What kinds of sins did we have?

[The original sin and sins we commit by ourselves.]

4. How can the problem of sin be resolved?

[When we repent of our sins and accept the Lord Jesus Christ, we can be redeemed from our sins by the redemptive blood of Jesus Christ.]

5. What is the meaning in the 'Regeneration' among the five-fold gospel?

[It refers to being born of the water and the Holy Spirit. It means we are born again, from the sinners to the righteous, by being washed by the blood of Jesus Christ through repentance.]

6. What is the meaning in the 'Sanctification' in the five-fold gospel?

[It means those who are born again cast off sins and evil and live by the Word of God to cultivate holiness by the help of the Holy Spirit.]

7. What is the meaning in the 'Divine Healing' in the five-fold gospel?

[It refers to being healed of sickensses and infirmities by the power of God.]

8. What is the meaning in the 'Resurrection' in the five-fold gospel?

[It refers to being raised again from death. Just as Jesus broke the authority of death and resurrected, God's children will resurrect into a spiritual body which can live forever.]

9. What is the meaning in the 'Second Advent' in the five-fold gospel?

[It refers to the Lord's coming back in just the same way He went up into Heaven.]

10. Do you believe that God did not predestine those who will be saved, but the salvation is up to each one's choice of faith?

[Yes]

11. Do you admit that each individual has different measure of faith and are you willing to try your best to attain to higher levels of faith?

[Yes]

12. What do we have to cut off in the world to love God according to the word found 1 John 2:16?

[The lust of the flesh, the lust of the eyes, and the boastful pride of this life]

13. How can we get rid of the sins that God hates?

[Along with our own effort to cast off sins, we have to receive the grace and strength of God and help of the Holy Spirit through fervent prayers.]

14. What are the sins leading to death?

[First, speaking against, opposing, hindering and disgracing the Holy Spirit (Matthew 12:31-32; Mark 3:29; Luke 12:10); second, crucifying the Lord again and putting Him to open shame (Hebrews 6:4-6); and third, going on sinning willfully after receiving the knowledge of the truth (Hebrews 10:26-27)]

"Therefore I say to you, any sin and blasphemy shall be forgiven people, but blasphemy against the Spirit shall not be forgiven. Whoever speaks a word against the Son of Man, it shall be forgiven him; but whoever speaks against the Holy Spirit, it shall not be forgiven him, either in this age or in the age to come." (Matthew 12:31-32)

"But whoever blasphemes against the Holy Spirit never has forgiveness, but is guilty of an eternal sin." (Mark 3:29)

"And everyone who speaks a word against the Son of Man, it will be forgiven him; but he who blasphemes against the Holy Spirit, it will not be forgiven him." (Luke 12:10)

"For in the case of those who have once been enlightened and have tasted of the heavenly gift and have been made partakers of the Holy Spirit, and have tasted the good word of God and the powers of the age to come, and then have fallen away, it is impossible to renew them again to repentance, since they again crucify to themselves the Son of God and put Him to open shame." (Hebrews 6:4-6)

"For if we go on sinning willfully after receiving the knowledge of the truth, there no longer remains a sacrifice for sins, but a terrifying expectation of judgment and the fury of a fire which will consume the adversaries." (Hebrews 10:26-27)

15. Do you know that salvation is renounced from those who practice the evident deeds/works of the flesh recorded in Galatians 5:19-21?

[Yes]

16. Do you know the Holy Spirit who has entered our hearts may be quenched when we commit sins?

[Yes]

17. What is the grace?

[Grace refers to what is given freely by God. God gives us all things we need in our lives, and He also gives us eternal life by forgiving us of our sins through Jesus Christ.]

18. What is the baptism of water?

[The baptism of water is one of the sacraments of the church, which is a symbolical sign of being forgiven of our sins and becoming a child of God. It also means we have to keep on cleansing ourselves by meditating on the Word of God which is the truth.]

19. What is the baptism of the Holy Spirit?

[When we repent of our sins and accept Jesus Christ, the Holy Spirit comes into our heart and revives our dead spirit. This reviving of our dead spirit is the baptism of the Holy Spirit.]

20. What is the baptism of fire of the Holy Spirit?

[It is to receive the fire of the Holy Spirit and to be given the strength of God. When we receive the baptism of fire of the Holy Spirit, it scorches sinful natures and diseases and drives away the enemy devil and Satan from our homes, work places and business fields.]

21. What is the Holy Communion?

[It is a sacrament in which we eat the bread symbolizing the body of Jesus and drink the cup symbolizing His blood. It is to commemorate Jesus' love in dying on the cross for us and giving out all His flesh and blood. Furthermore, it reminds us of what kind of Christian life we have to live in order to gain eternal life.]

22. Where does the Holiness Church have its roots?

[It is based on the holiness movement of John Wesley in the United Kingdom during the 18th century.]

23. Recite the Lord's Prayer recorded in Matthew 6:9-13.

[Our Father, who art in heaven, hallowed be Thy name. Thy Kingdom come, Thy will be done on earth as it is in heaven. Give us this day our daily bread. And forgive us our trespasses, as we have forgiven those who trespassed against us. And lead us not into temptation, but deliver us from evil. For Thine is the kingdom, and the power, and the glory, forever and ever. Amen.]

24. What is the Apostles' Creed?

[It is the summation of all the fundamental doctrines of Christianity, and the confession of Christian faith.]

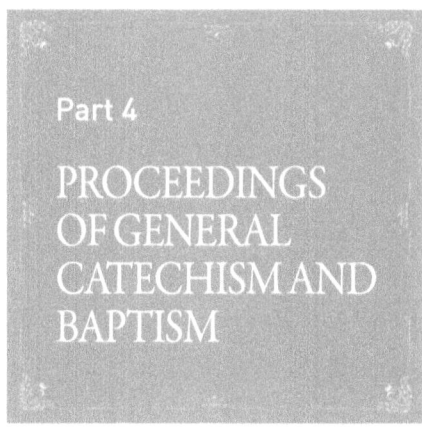

Part 4

PROCEEDINGS
OF GENERAL
CATECHISM AND
BAPTISM

General Catechism

Baptism

Chapter 1 — General Catechism

* Those who will be catechismal members will sit before the podium and conduct the catechism ceremony according to the following proceedings.

1. Hymnal Song

2. Prayer

3. Passage Reading (Ephesians 4:17-24)

4. Call the names of going-to-be catechismal
   members and let them stand up

5. Ceremonial Address

Dear brothers and sisters in Christ, we will have the Ceremony for the General Catechism according to the constitution of the church. We have this ceremony of general catechism for the newly jointed brothers and sisters in order to give them more training on having deep experience of faith, knowledge of the Bible, and the service for the church. All the other brothers and sisters should set a good example with love, faith, and purity in their words and deeds, and keep the truth of the Bible and the laws of the church.

6. Questions and Answers

Dear brothers and sisters, we know that you have already departed from sins and evil, and that you believe in the Lord Jesus Christ and serve God. Now please give your sincere answers to the following questions to show your resolution to God and the church.

Question 1:

Are you willing to repent of all your sins, cast off all former ways of your life and all kinds of bad habits, and believe in the Lord Jesus as your Savior?

[Amen]

Question 2:

Are you willing to believe the Bible is the Word of God, live according to the teachings of the Bible, and keep the Ten Commandments?

[Amen]

Question 3:

Are you willing to read the Bible and pray diligently and make effort to evangelize others?

[Amen]

Question 4:

Do you want to dwell in the grace of regeneration, the foundation of Christian truth, and are you willing to obey the Word of God and the guidance of the Holy Spirit in your faith and deeds?

[Amen]

Question 5:

On the Lord's Day, are you willing to quit all worldly works, worship God in a godly manner, and voluntarily render service to the church, the body of the Christ in spirit and in flesh?

[Amen]

7. Proclamation

Since all brothers and sisters here in attendance declared their resolution before God and the church by giving their sincere answers to the given questions, we proclaim they have become catechismal members of _____ church, of the United Holiness Church of Jesus Christ.

8. After prayer, it goes on to baptism. If there is no one to be baptised, it will be closed with a hymnal and benediction.

Chapter 2

Baptism

Baptism is principally supposed to be held at a river or a baptismal pool. But, when the situation or conditions do not allow for it, the baptism ceremony may be conducted according to the following procedures.

1. Hymn

2. Opening Prayer

3. Passage Reading (John 3:1-8)

4. Ceremonial Address

Baptism is a sacrament commanded by the Lord, and you are here at this ceremony to be baptized with water according to the command of the Lord. Now I pray that the mercy and blessings of God will be revealed to you brothers and sisters, so that you will gain the qualification to enter the heavenly kingdom and enjoy eternal life as perfect children of God.

5. Prayer for the Catechism for Baptism

6. Call the names of those who are to be baptized for them to stand up.

7. Questions and Answers

Dear brothers and sisters in Christ, you have come here to be baptized with water, and please give your sincere answers to the following questions before God and the church.

Question 1:

Are you willing to repent of your sins, and cast off your old manners of life and ungodly habits, and do you believe that you become children of God by being born again through the faith in Jesus Christ as your personal Savior?

[Amen]

Question 2:

Do you believe that you will receive the grace of sanctification through the precious blood of Jesus Christ and the power of the Holy Spirit after experiencing the grace of regeneration?

[Amen]

Question 3:

Do you completely believe in the Apostles' Creed as the foundation of your faith?

[Amen]

Question 4:

Do you believe you will become united with the Lord through baptism, and are you willing to live to the glory of the Lord during all the days of your life whether you eat or drink or whatever you do?

[Amen]

Question 5:

Are you willing to read the Bible, pray, evangelize, give tithes and offerings, keep the Lord's Day holy, and faithfully serve the church in every aspect?

[Amen]

8. Prayer for the Baptism

9. Baptism

I baptize _____ in the name of God the Father, God the Son, and God the Holy Spirit, Amen.

10. Proclamation

I proclaim that these brothers and sisters have given their sincere answers to all the given questions and been baptized in the name of God the Trinity, and thus have become baptized members of _____ Church, of the United Holiness Church of Jesus Christ.

11. Prayer

12. Advice

APPENDIX

The Roles of the Church Established in the Name of the Lord Jesus Christ

Overview on the Old and New Testaments

The Roles of the Church Established in the Name of the Lord Jesus Christ

When Peter confessed to Jesus, *"You are the Christ, the Son of the living God,"* Jesus said, *"I also say to you that you are Peter, and upon this rock I will build My church; and the gates of Hades will not overpower it. I will give you the keys of the kingdom of heaven; and whatever you bind on earth shall have been bound in heaven, and whatever you loose on earth shall have been loosed in heaven"* (Matthew 16:16-19).

From that time, Jesus spoke to His disciples about His Passion, crucifixion, and resurrection, and He finally fulfilled God's providence as the Savior. After His ascension, the Holy Spirit came down onto His disciples and they spread the gospel to Jerusalem, all regions of Judea, Samaria, and even to the ends of the earth, and many churches have been established at all corners of the globe.

There are various types of churches in the world according to the Lord's letters to seven churches as recorded in Revelation chapter 2 and 3. The letters are the Lord's most earnest desire to awaken all the churches that have existed, both in the past and in present. Let us delve into an ideal church based on the Biblical teachings.

The fundamental reason for us to attend church is to gain salvation. Since the wages of sin is death as recorded in Romans 6:23, we can gain complete salvation only when the problem of our sins is resolved. So, the church must explain to the church members how terrible sins are, why we cannot be saved because of our sins, and why we must cast off our sins. When we hear the gospel and accept Jesus Christ, our names are recorded in the book of life in Heaven. But this is the beginning of our salvation. Our salvation is perfected at the moment when we meet the Lord.

Some believers may ask, "I have already accepted the Lord and been forgiven of all my sins committed in the past, the present and the future. Why should I be convicted of my sins continually and be told to repent of those sins?" It's because accepting the Lord is the beginning of salvation and we should keep our salvation complete by the help of the church. Our car's entering a highway doesn't mean we have arrived at the destination. Similarly, after accepting the Lord and being forgiven of our sins, we should be born of water and the Spirit (John 3:5) and eat the flesh and drink the blood of the Son of Man (John 6:53). In other words, we should continually keep and obey the Word of God and attain to the complete salvation.

Second, the church members' faith must be increasing and they must become God's true and holy children.

The Lord saved us with His great love through His crucifixion, and thus none of us should think like, 'Now I have been saved, so I'll lead my own life as my heart desires'. The way to pay back for this grace of God is to love God, and to perform the duty worthy for the children of God. If we attend church but do not get rid of sinful natures from within our hearts, we may commit sins. Then, various problems happen to us at our homes, businesses and places of work. They also have an effect on our health.

In this sense, it is important to cast off sinful natures that cause us to commit sins in action, even if sins are not yet revealed in deeds. Therefore, we should throw away the lust of the flesh, the lust of the eyes, and the boastful pride of this life, and become sanctified. Then, we can restore the lost image of God and come forth as Christ-like children of God. In brief, a new believer who has just received salvation has to increase his faith up to the full measure of the Christ—the most matured faith in which he is never shaken in any circumstances.

Third, the church should proclaim the Lord who will come again.

Those who believe they know at which point in time the Lord would come again be fixated with the time limit. It is difficult for them to lead a normal social and family life. But true significance of eschatology is not to have a fixed time frame but to prepare ourselves to meet the Lord, no matter when God calls our spirit or when the Lord would come again.

Therfore, the church should teach a good eschatology so that the believers can be on the alert and lead a proper Christian life. To attend a church that teaches the members to prepare for the second coming of the Lord and to attend a church that does not are completely different from each other. The parable of ten virgins in Matthew 25 tells us that the ten virgins knew the fact of the coming of the bridegroom but only five of them prepared oil. The church should teach the believers to prepare for the life after death and wait for the second coming of the Lord.

Fourth, the church should let the believers meet and experience God.

If some attend church for 10 or 20 years but have never met God, they should examine whether or not their churches have the presence of God. We believers pray to meet and experience God not because we have no faith but because we have faith. God promises, *"Ask, and it will be given to you; seek, and you will find; knock, and it will be opened to you"* (Matthew 7:7). God meets those who earnestly seek Him.

An elementary school student wouldn't understand the depth of the college mathmatics. It is the same in faith. If a new believer who has little knowledge of spirit tries to measure and understand the spiritual realm with physical knowledge, it is absurd. If he humbly learns and tries to accept it little by little, he will be able to understand it fully. So, if we understand and believe the works of God in our heart, we will naturally understand it with our head, too. Then, we can experience works of God.

Fifth, the church should lead the believers to trust and follow the shepherd that God appoints for the church.

God establishes both His church, the body of Christ, and the shepherd of the church. God appoints the shepherds because the Lord Himself cannot come to this earth and rule over all churches. The apostle Paul said in 2 Corinthians 12:12, *"The signs of a true apostle were performed among you with all perseverance, by signs and wonders and miracles."*

A shepherd can be proven to have been established by God through all perseverance, signs, wonders, and miracles. If church members do not trust such a shepherd, they should examine how sincerely they have tried their best to practice the Word of God and how deeply they have felt God's love. To trust the shepherd established for the church, the body of the Christ, is to believe and turst God, too.

Overview on the Old and New Testaments

The Bible had been written over a period of about 1,600 years from the time of Moses until the first century. Approximately 40 people recorded it by the inspiration of the Holy Spirit. The Bible consists of 66 books—39 books of the Old Testament and 27 books of the New Testament. Since you have completed the catechsim or been baptized, why don't you try to read the whole Bible after understanding the main flow of the Old and New Testaments?

The 39 books of the Old Testament were mostly written in Hebrew, and a few were written in Aramaic, while the 27 books of the New Testament were written in Greek. Until the printing press was invented in 1456, the manuscripts of the Bible were all copied by handwriting and distributed. After the Reformation, the Bible began to be translated into many languages and read by many people.

The New Testament consists of the Four Gospels, one historical book, twenty-one Epistles, and one prophetic book. The Old Testament has 17 historical books, 5 poetic books and 17 prophetic books.

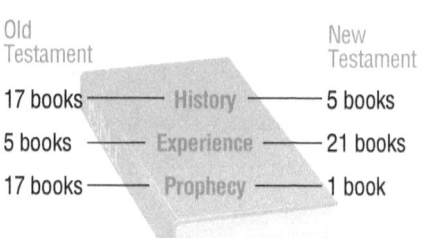

Old Testament		New Testament
17 books	History	5 books
5 books	Experience	21 books
17 books	Prophecy	1 book

The 66 books of the Bible has 1,189 chapters. If we read a chapter every day, it takes more than three years to read the whole Bible. If we read three chapters a day, it takes more than a year. So, if we read three chapters every day and five chapters on every Sunday, we can finish reading the whole Bible in a year.

The Old Testament in Chronological Order

We can understand the Old Testament more easily with the understanding of the history. First, we can understand the backbone structure of the Old Testament with the 11 history books. Then, if we understand which poetic books and which prophetic books were written at which point in the history, it is easier to understand the Old Testament.

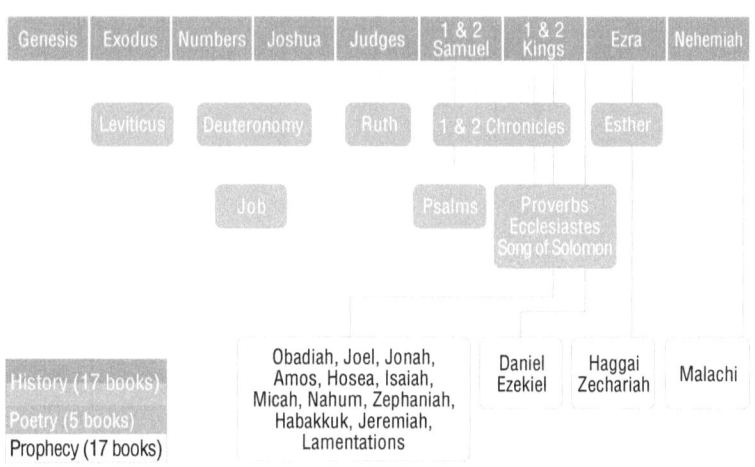

< Categories of the Historical Books According to the Chronology >

Era of Creation	Genesis 1 through 11
Era of Patriarch	Genesis 12 through 50
Era of Moses	Exodus, Leviticus, Numbers, Deuteronomy
Era of Judges	Joshua, Judges, Ruth, 1 Samuel 1 through 15
Era of Monarchy	1 Samuel 16 through 31, 2 Samuel, 1 & 2 Kings, 1 & 2 Chronicles
Era of Captivity	Ezra, Nehemiah, Esther

The New Testament in Chronological Order

The 27 books of the New Testament are not arranged in chronological order. Thus, if we categorize the 27 books in chronological order before we read each book, we can understand the flow of the New Testament more easily.

The Four Gospels record Jesus' ministires and they represent the era of Jesus Christ. The Acts of the Apostles and the Espistles record the formation of churches and the ministries of the apostles, and they represent the era of the Holy Spirit, the era of the churches.

The Revelation of John in detail write about the things to come, such as the coming of the Lord in the air, the Seven-year Wedding Banquet and Tribulation, the Lord's second coming to the earth, the Millennium Kingdom, and the Great White Throne Judgment.

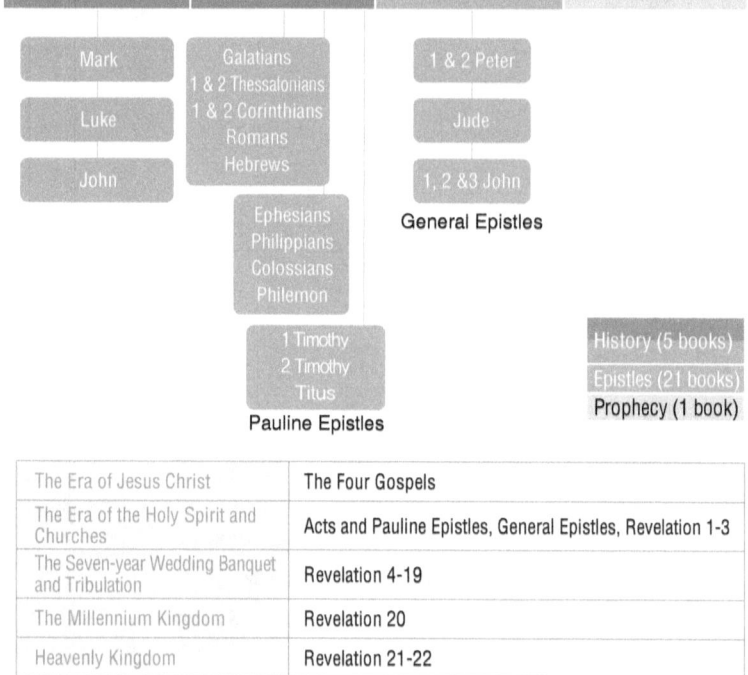

The Era of Jesus Christ	The Four Gospels
The Era of the Holy Spirit and Churches	Acts and Pauline Epistles, General Epistles, Revelation 1-3
The Seven-year Wedding Banquet and Tribulation	Revelation 4-19
The Millennium Kingdom	Revelation 20
Heavenly Kingdom	Revelation 21-22

"You will receive power when the Holy Spirit has come upon you;
and you shall be My witnesses both in Jerusalem,
and in all Judea and Samaria, and even to the remotest part of the earth."

(Acts 1:8)

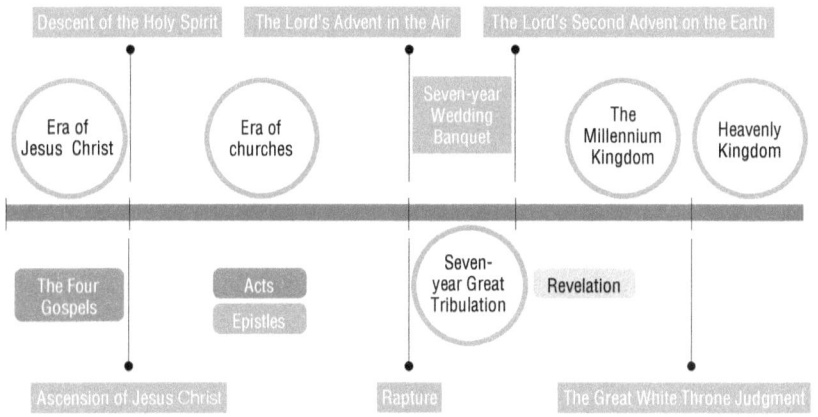

"Behold, I am coming quickly, and My reward is with Me,
to render to every man according to what he has done."

(Revelation 22:12)

The Author
Dr. Jaerock Lee

Dr. Jaerock Lee was born in Muan, Jeonnam Province, Republic of Korea, in 1943. In his twenties, he suffered from a variety of incurable diseases for seven years and awaited death with no hope for recovery. One day in the spring of 1974, however, he was led to a church by his sister, and when he knelt down to pray, the living God immediately healed him of all his diseases.

From the moment Dr. Lee met the living God through that wonderful experience, he has loved God with all his heart and sincerity, and in 1978 was called to be a servant of God. He prayed fervently so that he could clearly understand the will of God and wholly accomplish it, and obeyed all the word of God. In 1982, he founded Manmin Church in Seoul, S. Korea, and countless works of God, including miraculous healings and wonders, have been taking place at his church.

In 1986, Dr. Lee was ordained as a pastor at the Annual Assembly of Jesus' Sungkyul Church of Korea, and four years later in 1990, his sermons began to be broadcast on the Far East Broadcasting Company, the Asia Broadcast Station, and the Washington Christian Radio System to Australia, Russia, the Philippines, and many more.

Three years later in 1993, Manmin Central Church was selected as one of the "World's Top 50 Churches" by the *Christian World* magazine (US) and he received an Honorary Doctorate of Divinity from Christian Faith College, Florida, USA, and in 1996 a Ph. D. in Ministry from Kingsway Theological Seminary, Iowa, USA.

Since 1993, Dr. Lee has been spearheading world evangelization through many overseas crusades in Tanzania, Argentina, L.A., Baltimore City, Hawaii, and New York City of the USA, Uganda, Japan, Pakistan, Kenya, the Philippines, Honduras, India, Russia, Germany, Peru, Democratic Republic of the Congo, Israel and Estonia.

In 2002 he was called a "worldwide revivalist" by major Christian newspapers in Korea for his powerful ministries in various overseas crusades. Especially, his

'New York Crusade 2006' held in Madison Square Garden, the most world-famous arena, was broadcast to 220 nations, and in his 'Israel United Crusade 2009' held in International Convention Center in Jerusalem he boldly proclaimed Jesus Christ is the Messiah and Savior. His sermon is brodacst to 176 nations via satellites including GCN TV and he was listed as one of the Top 10 Most Influential Christian Leaders of 2009 and 2010 by the Russian popular Christian magazine *In Victory* and new agency *Christian Telegraph* for his powerful TV broadcasting ministry and overseas church-pastoring ministry.

As of November 2011, Manmin Central Church is a congregation of more than 120,000 members and has 9,000 branch churches throughout the globe including 54 domestic branch churches in major cities, and has so far commissioned more than 137 missionaries to 23 countries, including the United States, Russia, Germany, Canada, Japan, China, France, India, Kenya, and many more.

To this day, Dr. Lee has written 64 books, including bestsellers *Tasting Eternal Life before Death, My Life My Faith I & II, The Message of the Cross, The Measure of Faith, Heaven I & II,* and *Hell,* and his works have been being translated into more than 71 languages.

His Christian columns appear on *The Hankook Ilbo, The JoongAng Daily, The Chosun Ilbo, The Dong-A Ilbo, The Munhwa Ilbo, The Seoul Shinmun, The Kyunghyang Shinmun, The Hankyoreh Shinmun, The Korea Economic Daily, The Korea Herald, The Shisa News, The Christian Press.*

Dr. Lee is currently leader of many missionary organizations and associations including: Chairman, The United Holiness Church of Jesus Christ; Permanent President of the World Christianity Revival Mission Association; President, Manmin World Mission; Founder, Manmin TV; Founder & Board Chairman, Global Christian Network (GCN); Founder & Board Chairman, World Christian Doctors Network (WCDN); and Founder & Board Chairman, Manmin International Seminary (MIS).

Other powerful books by this author

Heaven I & II

A detailed sketch of the gorgeous living environment the heavenly citizens enjoy and beautiful description of different levels of heavenly kingdoms.

The Message of the Cross

A powerful awakening message for all the people who are spiritually asleep! In this book you will find the reason Jesus is the only Savior and the true love of God.

Hell

An earnest message to all mankind from God, who wishes not even one soul to fall into the depths of hell! You will discover the never-before-revealed account of the cruel reality of the Lower Grave and Hell.

Tasting Eternal Life Before Death

A testimonial memoirs of Dr. Jaerock Lee, who was born again and saved from the valley of death and has been leading an exemplary Christian life.

The Measure of Faith

What kind of a dwelling place, crown and reward are prepared for you in heaven? This book provides with wisdom and guidance for you to measure your faith and cultivate the best and most mature faith.

Awaken, Israel

Why has God kept His eyes on Israel from the beginning of the world to this day? What kind of His providence has been prepared for Israel in the last days, who await the Messiah?

My Life My Faith I & II

Dr. Jaerock Lee's autobiography provides the most fragrant spiritual aroma for the readers, through his life extracted from the love of God blossomed in midst of the dark waves, cold yoke and the deepest despair.

The Power of God

A must-read that serves as an essential guide by which one can possess true faith and experience the wondrous power of God.

Other powerful books by this author

Man of Flesh, Man of Spirit I & II

A detailed scrutiny about the evil and sinful nature deep within our heart through Job's sickness, sufferings, and healing and recovery, and the methodology on how to change into men of spirit.

Lectures on the First Corinthians I & II

A guidebook accounting for basics of Christians and various life problems including lawsuits, strife, marriage, idolatry, and the spiritual gifts and for the victory in spiritual warfare.

Seven Churches

The Lord's earnest messages awakening believers and churches from spiritual slumber, sent to the seven churches recorded in Revelation chapter 2 and 3, which refer to all the churches of the Lord.

Footsteps of the Lord I & II

An unraveled account of secrets about the beginning of time, the origin of Jesus, and God's providence and love for allowing His only begotten Son Passion and resurrection!

God the Healer

A milestone to lead us to fundamental healing and a healthy life freedom from sickness and disease, and to explain about the original cause of diseases and divine healing according to biblical principles.

Keep Watching and Praying

Prayer is a key to knock and unlock the door to the heart of the almighty God and a weapon to defeat the enemy devil and be victorious in the spiritual world, and the way to lucidly understand His will and live by it.

The Law of God

If you come to know the deep love of God embedded in the Ten Commandments you will find the way of drawing yourself close to God, of receiving answers from God, and of abiding with God.

A Man Who Pursues True Blessing

Jesus' message titled with "Beatitudes" helps us realize what true blessing is so that we will not only enjoy all the blessings of this world including wealth, health, fame, and authority, but possess New Jerusalem.

www.ingramcontent.com/pod-product-compliance
Lightning Source LLC
Chambersburg PA
CBHW020425130626
46549CB00006B/2740